healthy

simple and delicious
easy-to-make lowfat recipes

Susanna Tee

p

This is a Parragon Publishing Book
This edition published in 2004

Parragon Publishing
Queen Street House
4 Queen Street
Bath, BA1 1HE, UK

Copyright © Exclusive Editions 2002

ISBN: 1-40543-642-5

Printed in China

Produced by
THE BRIDGEWATER BOOK COMPANY LTD

Photographer: Ian Parsons
Home Economist: Sara Hesketh

Cover Photography: Calvey Taylor-Haw
Home Economist: Ruth Pollock

NOTES FOR THE READER

- This book uses imperial, metric, and cup measurements. Follow the same units of measurement throughout; do not mix imperial and metric.

- All spoon measurements are level: teaspoons are assumed to be 5 ml, and tablespoons are assumed to be 15 ml.

- Unless otherwise stated, milk is assumed to be whole milk, eggs and individual vegetables such as potatoes are medium, and pepper is freshly ground black pepper.

- Recipes using raw or very lightly cooked eggs should be avoided by infants, the elderly, pregnant women, convalescents, and anyone suffering from an illness.

- The times given are an approximate guide only. Preparation times differ according to the techniques used by different people and the cooking times may also vary from those given. Optional ingredients, variations, or serving suggestions have not been included in the calculations.

contents

introduction

This book will convince you that a healthy lowfat diet need never be dreary. These dishes are bursting with flavor. All are easy to prepare and good to eat. There are no complicated cooking methods involved or expensive ingredients to buy.

To keep healthy your body needs a balanced diet. You can see what each of these recipes is made up of by checking its nutritional information. The recipes use fat-free or fat-reduced cooking methods, and all you need to do is to select lowfat dairy products, lean meats, such as skinless chicken and turkey, and the leanest cuts of beef, lamb, and pork, and of course, plenty of vegetables.

Vegetable oil spray also reduces the amount of fat used, for example when stir-frying, and nonstick liner is useful for lining cookie sheets. The only special equipment you need is a heavy, nonstick skillet or a nonstick wok.

chicken & vegetable soup
page 12

quick-fried pork & pears
page 58

When serving bread or vegetables with these dishes, don't be tempted to reach for the butter dish. Simply eat delicious fresh bread on its own and add a generous sprinkling of chopped herbs to the vegetables. Instead of buying rich salad dressings, make your own dressings using lowfat yogurt or cottage cheese, or use a fat-reduced mayonnaise. You will soon be feeling healthier without feeling deprived of your favorite dishes.

Key to Recipes

easy

Recipes are graded as follows:
1 spoon = easy;
2 spoons = very easy;
3 spoons = extremely easy.

serves 4

Recipes generally serve four people. Simply halve the ingredients to serve two, taking care not to mix metric and imperial measurements.

15 minutes

Preparation time. Where marinating or soaking are involved, these times have been added on separately: eg, 15 minutes + 30 minutes to marinate.

40 minutes

Cooking time. Cooking times do not include the cooking of side dishes or accompaniments served with the main dishes.

penne primavera
page 68

apple & honey water ice
page 90

These are recipes that are easy to make yet satisfying to eat at a midday break or as a light evening meal. They are ideal served simply with fresh crusty bread and then followed with fresh fruit for a healthy lunch or supper. Most of them—for example, Sweet Red Bell Pepper & Tomato Soup, and Greek Feta Salad—can also be served as an appetizer because they are light and refreshing. Choose from delicious temptations such as Chilled Smoked Mackerel with Horseradish Dressing, Shrimp & Mango Salad, and Vegetable Frittata.

light lunches
& suppers

sweet red bell pepper & tomato soup

extremely
easy

serves 4

5 minutes

30–35
minutes

ingredients

1 tbsp olive oil

2 tbsp water

2 red bell peppers, seeded
  and chopped finely

1 garlic clove, chopped finely

1 onion, chopped finely

14 oz/400 g canned
  chopped tomatoes

5 cups vegetable bouillon

salt and pepper

fresh basil leaves, to garnish

NUTRITIONAL INFORMATION	
calories	89
protein	3 g
carbohydrate	12 g
sugars	10 g
fat	4 g
saturates	0.5 g

Put the oil, water, bell peppers, garlic, and onion in a pan, heat gently, and cook for 5–10 minutes, or until the vegetables have softened. Cover the pan and simmer for a further 10 minutes.

Add the tomatoes, bouillon, salt, and pepper and simmer, uncovered, for 15 minutes.

Serve garnished with basil leaves.

mixed bean soup

extremely easy

serves 4

10 minutes   35 minutes

ingredients

1 garlic clove, crushed
1 onion, chopped finely
1 celery stalk, sliced finely
1 carrot, diced finely
1 leek, sliced finely
14 oz/400 g canned
  chopped tomatoes
2½ cups vegetable bouillon

salt and pepper
pinch of dried mixed herbs
14 oz/400 g canned red kidney beans,
  drained and rinsed
14 oz/400 g black-eye peas, drained
  and rinsed

warm crusty bread, to serve

NUTRITIONAL INFORMATION	
calories	238
protein	16 g
carbohydrate	42 g
sugars	11 g
fat	2 g
saturates	neg

Put all the ingredients, except the beans, into a large pan. Bring to a boil, then simmer for 30 minutes, stirring occasionally, until the vegetables are tender.

Add the beans and simmer for a further 4–5 minutes, or until hot.

Serve with warm crusty bread.

chicken & vegetable soup

ingredients

extremely easy   serves 4

10 minutes   1 hour 10 minutes

1 onion, chopped finely

1 garlic clove, chopped finely

1¼ cups shredded white cabbage

2 carrots, chopped finely

4 potatoes, diced

1 green bell pepper, seeded and diced

14 oz/400 g canned chopped tomatoes

5⅔ cups chicken bouillon

salt and pepper

1¼ cups diced cooked chicken

chopped fresh parsley, to garnish

warm crusty bread, to serve

NUTRITIONAL INFORMATION	
calories	89
protein	3 g
carbohydrate	12 g
sugars	10 g
fat	4 g
saturates	0.5 g

Put all the ingredients, except the chicken and parsley, in a large pan and bring to a boil. Simmer for 1 hour, or until the vegetables are tender.

Add the chicken and simmer for a further 10 minutes, or until hot.

Garnish with parsley and serve with warm crusty bread.

tuna & fresh vegetable salad

extremely easy

serves 4

10 minutes
+ 1 hour
to marinate

ingredients

DRESSING
4 tbsp reduced-calorie mayonnaise
4 tbsp lowfat plain yogurt
2 tbsp white wine vinegar
salt and pepper

12 cherry tomatoes, halved
1 ½ cups whole green beans,
  cut into 1-inch/2.5-cm pieces

8 oz/225 g zucchini, sliced thinly
3¼ cups thinly sliced
  white mushrooms
12 oz/350 g canned tuna in brine,
  drained and flaked

chopped fresh parsley, to garnish

salad greens, to serve

NUTRITIONAL INFORMATION	
calories	187
protein	26 g
carbohydrate	8 g
sugars	7 g
fat	6 g
saturates	0.5 g

To make the dressing, put the mayonnaise, yogurt, vinegar, salt, and pepper in a screw-topped jar and shake together until the ingredients are well blended.

Put the tomatoes, beans, zucchini, and mushrooms in a bowl. Pour over the dressing and marinate for about 1 hour.

To serve, arrange the salad greens on a serving dish. Add the vegetables and then the tuna, and garnish with parsley.

greek feta salad

extremely easy

serves 4

10 minutes

DRESSING
3 tbsp extra virgin olive oil
1 tbsp lemon juice
½ tsp dried oregano
salt and pepper

4 tomatoes, sliced
½ cucumber, peeled and sliced
1 small red onion, sliced thinly
4 oz/115 g feta cheese, cubed
8 black olives

a few grape leaves, to serve

NUTRITIONAL INFORMATION	
calories	186
protein	6 g
carbohydrate	7 g
sugars	6 g
fat	15 g
saturates	5 g

To make the dressing, put the oil, lemon juice, oregano, salt, and pepper in a screw-topped jar and shake together until blended.

Arrange the grape leaves on a serving dish and then the tomatoes, cucumber, and onion. Sprinkle the cheese and olives on top. Pour the dressing over the salad and serve.

shrimp & mango salad

extremely easy

serves 4

10 minutes

2 mangoes

2 cups peeled, cooked shrimp

1 tbsp lemon juice

salt and pepper

DRESSING

juice from the mangoes

6 tbsp lowfat plain yogurt

2 tbsp reduced-calorie mayonnaise

4 whole cooked shrimp, to garnish

salad greens, to serve

NUTRITIONAL INFORMATION	
calories	146
protein	16 g
carbohydrate	15 g
sugars	14 g
fat	3 g
saturates	0.5 g

Cutting close to the pit, cut a large slice from one side of each mango, then cut another slice from the opposite side. Without breaking the skin, cut the flesh in the segments into squares, then push the skin inside out to expose the cubes, and cut away from the skin. Use a sharp knife to peel the remaining center section and cut the flesh away from the pit into cubes. Reserve any juice in a bowl and put the mango flesh in a separate bowl.

Add the shrimp to the mango flesh. Add the yogurt, mayonnaise, lemon juice, salt, and pepper to the juice and blend together.

Arrange the salad greens on a serving dish and add the mango flesh and shrimp. Pour the dressing over them and serve garnished with the shrimp.

warm chicken liver salad

very easy   serves 4

5 minutes   10–12
minutes

ingredients

salad greens
1 tbsp olive oil
1 small onion, chopped finely
1 lb/450 g frozen chicken livers, thawed

1 tsp chopped fresh tarragon
1 tsp wholegrain mustard
2 tbsp balsamic vinegar
salt and pepper

NUTRITIONAL INFORMATION	
calories	142
protein	21 g
carbohydrate	2 g
sugars	1 g
fat	6 g
saturates	1 g

Arrange the salad greens on serving plates.

Heat the oil in a nonstick skillet, add the onion, and cook for 5 minutes, or until softened. Add the chicken livers, tarragon, and mustard and cook for 3–5 minutes, stirring, until tender. Put on top of the salad greens.

Add the vinegar, salt, and pepper to the skillet and heat, stirring constantly, until all the sediment has been lifted from the skillet. Pour the dressing over the chicken livers and serve warm.

chilled smoked mackerel
with horseradish dressing

extremely
easy

serves 4

10 minutes
+ at least
30 minutes
to chill

ingredients

4 smoked mackerel

sprigs of watercress or mizuna, to garnish

DRESSING
⅔ cup lowfat plain yogurt
1 tsp grated horseradish
salt and pepper

NUTRITIONAL INFORMATION	
calories	376
protein	21 g
carbohydrate	3 g
sugars	3 g
fat	31 g
saturates	6 g

Remove the skin from the mackerel fillets, then cut each fillet in half lengthwise. Chill in the refrigerator for at least 30 minutes.

Meanwhile, combine the yogurt, horseradish, salt, and pepper. Chill in the refrigerator with the mackerel.

To serve, arrange the mackerel on serving plates, spoon the horseradish dressing over it, and garnish with watercress sprigs or mizuna.

vegetable frittata

easy   serves 4

10 minutes   20–30
              minutes

ingredients

4 eggs
2 egg whites
salt and pepper
1 tsp olive oil
1 onion, chopped coarsely
1 garlic clove, chopped finely
1 green bell pepper, seeded, cored,
    and chopped finely

1 zucchini, sliced thickly
8 oz/225 g cooked potatoes, diced
1 tomato, chopped coarsely
½ cup grated reduced-fat mozzarella

NUTRITIONAL INFORMATION	
calories	215
protein	13 g
carbohydrate	15 g
sugars	5 g
fat	12 g
saturates	4 g

Beat the whole eggs and egg whites in a bowl and season with salt and pepper.

Heat the oil in a large nonstick skillet and add the onion, garlic, and green bell pepper. Cook for 5 minutes, or until softened. Add the zucchini and potatoes and cook for a further 5–10 minutes, or until lightly browned. Stir in the tomato.

Pour in the egg mixture and cook over low heat for 5–10 minutes, or until the mixture is set and only the top is runny. Sprinkle the cheese over the top.

Transfer the pan to a preheated broiler and cook until the top is set, but not hard, and the cheese has melted and begun to brown. Serve hot, cut into wedges.

homemade turkey burgers

easy serves 8

15 minutes 20 minutes

i n g r e d i e n t s

¼ cup long-grain white rice
salt and pepper
1 lb/450 g lean ground turkey
1 small cooking apple, peeled,
  cored, and grated
1 small onion, chopped finely

1 garlic clove, chopped finely
1 tsp ground sage
½ tsp dried thyme
½ tsp ground allspice
vegetable oil spray, for frying

NUTRITIONAL INFORMATION	
calories	161
protein	26 g
carbohydrate	10 g
sugars	5 g
fat	2 g
saturates	1 g

Cook the rice in a large pan of boiling salted water for about 10 minutes, or until tender. Drain, rinse under cold running water, then drain well again.

Put the cooked rice and all the remaining ingredients in a large bowl and mix well together. With wet hands, shape the mixture into 8 thick burgers.

Spray a large, nonstick skillet with oil, add the burgers, and cook for about 10 minutes, turning them over several times, until they are golden brown. Remove from the skillet and serve while hot.

The following recipes show just how
easy it is to prepare healthy dishes.
They all use lean cuts of meat, poultry,
and fish that are seasoned with fresh
vegetables, herbs, and spices, and are
packed with flavor. There are recipes
for family meals and entertaining, and
recipes for warm summer evenings or
cold winter's nights. Choose from such
dishes as Moussaka, Chicken with a
Honey Glazed Crust, Marinated Lamb
Kabobs, and Broiled Salmon with
Red Bell Pepper Sauce. All are
mouthwatering—the only difficulty
is deciding which to choose!

main courses

mexican chicken burritos

very easy   serves 4

10 minutes   30 minutes

ingredients

8 wheat flour tortillas
vegetable oil spray
1 onion, chopped finely
4 skinless, boneless chicken breasts,
  sliced thinly

1 packet taco seasoning
4 tomatoes, chopped coarsely
4 scallions, sliced thinly

1 tub tomato salsa, to serve

NUTRITIONAL INFORMATION	
calories	473
protein	40 g
carbohydrate	75 g
sugars	7 g
fat	4 g
saturates	1 g

Preheat the oven to 300°F/150°C.

Wrap the tortillas in aluminum foil and cook in the oven for 10 minutes, or until soft.

Meanwhile, spray a large nonstick skillet with oil. Add the onion and cook for 5 minutes, or until softened. Add the chicken. Stirring occasionally, cook for 5 minutes, or until tender. Stir in the taco seasoning.

Preheat the oven to 350°F/180°C. Put the chicken mixture in the center of each tortilla and add the tomatoes and scallions. Fold the tortillas into a packet and put in an ovenproof dish.

Cover the dish and cook in the preheated oven for 20 minutes. Spoon the tomato salsa over the hot tortillas before serving.

chicken with a honey-glazed crust

very easy   serves 4

5 minutes   30–40 minutes

ingredients

3 tbsp wheat germ
3 tbsp honey
1 tbsp French mustard
4 skinless chicken breasts

salad greens (optional), to serve

NUTRITIONAL INFORMATION	
calories	194
protein	31 g
carbohydrate	13 g
sugars	12 g
fat	2 g
saturates	0.5 g

Preheat the oven to 375°F/190°C.

Put the wheat germ, honey, and mustard in a bowl and mix well together. Put the chicken breasts on a cookie sheet and spread with the honey mixture.

Bake the chicken in the oven for 30–40 minutes, or until the chicken is tender and a crust has formed. Remove from the oven and transfer to warm serving dishes.

Serve with salad greens, if you like.

italian braised chicken & fennel

very easy   serves 4

5 minutes   35 minutes

ingredients

4 tomatoes, chopped finely
1 garlic clove, crushed
¼ cup white wine
2 tsp balsamic vinegar
salt and pepper

4 skinless chicken breasts
4 small fennel bulbs, cut into fourths

flatleaf parsley, to garnish

NUTRITIONAL INFORMATION	
calories	166
protein	32 g
carbohydrate	5 g
sugars	5 g
fat	2 g
saturates	0.5 g

Put the tomatoes, garlic, wine, vinegar, salt, and pepper in a large, nonstick skillet and bring to a boil. Reduce the heat and add the chicken and fennel pieces. Cover and simmer for about 30 minutes, or until the chicken and fennel are tender.

Using a slotted spoon, transfer the chicken and fennel to warm serving plates.

Bring the sauce to a boil and cook, stirring occasionally, until thickened slightly. Spoon the sauce over the chicken and serve garnished with parsley.

tandoori chicken

very easy   serves 4

10 minutes
+ 24 hours
to marinate

45 minutes
to 1 hour

ingredients

4–8 skinless chicken breasts

MARINADE
1 small onion, cut into fourths
2 garlic cloves
1 tsp chopped fresh gingerroot
2 tsp ground cumin
2 tsp ground coriander

1 tsp garam masala
½ tsp salt
½ tsp cayenne pepper, optional
2 tbsp lemon or lime juice
4 tbsp lowfat plain yogurt
¼ tsp red food coloring

lemon or lime wedges, to garnish

NUTRITIONAL INFORMATION	
calories	160
protein	50 g
carbohydrate	4 g
sugars	3 g
fat	20 g
saturates	1 g

Using a sharp knife, cut ½-inch/1-cm deep slashes in each piece of chicken and put in a shallow dish.

Put all the remaining ingredients in a food processor and process until smooth. Spread the marinade over the chicken pieces, working it into the cuts in the flesh. Cover the dish and marinate in the refrigerator for 24 hours.

Preheat the oven to 400°F/200°C.

Place the chicken pieces on a rack in a roasting pan and cook in the oven for 45 minutes to 1 hour, turning the pieces over once and basting with the juices in the pan, until tender.

Serve garnished with lemon or lime wedges.

herb-crusted haddock with tomato salsa

very easy   serves 4

10 minutes   10–15
             minutes

ingredients

2 cups fresh white bread crumbs
3 tbsp lemon juice
1 tbsp pesto sauce
2 tbsp chopped fresh parsley
salt and pepper

vegetable oil spray
4 haddock fillets

1 tub tomato salsa, to serve

NUTRITIONAL
INFORMATION

calories	245
protein	41 g
carbohydrate	16 g
sugars	2 g
fat	2 g
saturates	0 g

Put the bread crumbs, 2 tablespoons of the lemon juice, the pesto sauce, parsley, salt, and pepper in a bowl and mix well together.

Line a broiler pan with aluminum foil and spray with vegetable oil. Place the haddock fillets on the foil and sprinkle with the remaining tablespoon of lemon juice and more salt and pepper. Cook under a preheated broiler for 5 minutes.

Turn the haddock fillets over and spread the herb and bread crumb mixture over the top of each.

Cook for a further 5–10 minutes, or until the haddock is tender and the crust is golden brown.

Serve with the tomato salsa spooned over the top of each fish.

broiled salmon with red bell pepper sauce

easy   serves 4

15 minutes   35–45 minutes

ingredients

3 red bell peppers
vegetable oil spray
4 salmon steaks
1 tbsp lemon juice
salt and pepper

1 onion, chopped finely
1 garlic clove, chopped finely
2 tsp balsamic vinegar
handful of fresh basil leaves

NUTRITIONAL INFORMATION	
calories	326
protein	32 g
carbohydrate	11 g
sugars	10 g
fat	17 g
saturates	3 g

Preheat the oven to 400°F/200°C.

Put the bell peppers on a cookie sheet and roast in the oven for 25 minutes, turning once, until deflated and slightly charred. Let cool, then peel off the skins and discard with the core and seeds.

Meanwhile, line a broiler pan with aluminum foil and spray with oil. Place the salmon steaks on the foil, sprinkle with lemon juice, salt, and pepper, and cook under a preheated broiler for 10–20 minutes, turning once, until tender.

Spray a small nonstick pan with oil and fry the onion and garlic for 5 minutes, or until softened. Process in a food processor with the bell pepper flesh, vinegar, basil, salt, and pepper until smooth. Return the mixture to the pan and reheat gently.

Serve the red bell pepper sauce with the cooked salmon steaks.

baked fish & fries

very easy　**serves 4**

20 minutes　40–45 minutes

ingredients

1 lb/450 g mealy potatoes, peeled and cut into thick, even French fries
vegetable oil spray
½ cup all-purpose white flour

1 egg
1 cup fresh white bread crumbs, seasoned with salt and pepper
4 cod or haddock fillets

NUTRITIONAL INFORMATION

calories	322
protein	37 g
carbohydrate	37 g
sugars	1 g
fat	4 g
saturates	1 g

Preheat the oven to 400°F/200°C. Line 2 cookie sheets with nonstick liner.

Rinse the sliced potatoes under cold running water, then dry well on a clean dish towel. Put in a bowl, spray with oil, and toss together until coated. Spread the fries on a cookie sheet and cook in the oven for 40–45 minutes, turning once, until golden.

Meanwhile, put the flour on a plate, beat the egg in a shallow dish, and spread the seasoned bread crumbs on a large plate. Dip the fish fillets in the flour to coat, then the egg, letting any excess drip off, and finally the bread crumbs, patting them firmly into the fish. Place the fish in a single layer on a cookie sheet.

Fifteen minutes before the fries have cooked, bake the fish fillets in the oven for 10–15 minutes, turning them once during cooking, until the fish is tender. Serve the fish with the fries.

red snapper with citrus fruit

very easy   serves 4

10 minutes   10–15
+ 4 hours   minutes
to marinate

ingredients

MARINADE
6 tbsp fresh orange juice
3 tbsp lemon juice
3 tbsp lime juice
4 tbsp dry sherry
1 tsp chopped garlic
1 tsp chopped fresh ginger
salt and pepper

vegetable oil spray, for frying
4 red snapper

orange segments, to garnish

NUTRITIONAL
INFORMATION

calories	194
protein	28 g
carbohydrate	3 g
sugars	3 g
fat	6 g
saturates	0 g

Put all the marinade ingredients in a shallow dish and mix them well together.

Using a sharp knife, slash the snapper 3 times on each side. Add the fish to the marinade and marinate in the refrigerator, turning once or twice, for about 4 hours.

Line a broiler pan with aluminum foil and spray with vegetable oil. Place the fish on the foil and cook under a preheated broiler for 10–15 minutes, turning once and spooning over the marinade, until the flesh is tender.

Serve garnished with orange segments.

flounder packets with fresh herbs

very easy   serves 4

10 minutes   15 minutes

ingredients

vegetable oil spray
4 flounder fillets, skinned
6 tbsp chopped fresh herbs,
    such as dill, parsley, chives,
    thyme, or marjoram

finely grated rind and juice
    of 2 lemons
1 small onion, sliced thinly
1 tbsp capers, rinsed (optional)
salt and pepper

NUTRITIONAL INFORMATION	
calories	129
protein	25 g
carbohydrate	2 g
sugars	1 g
fat	2 g
saturates	0 g

Preheat the oven to 375°F/190°C. Cut 4 large squares of aluminum foil, each large enough to hold a fish and form a packet, and spray with oil.

Place each fish fillet on a foil sheet and sprinkle them with the herbs, lemon rind and juice, onion, capers (if using), salt, and pepper. Fold the foil to make a secure packet and place on a cookie sheet.

Bake the packets in the oven for 15 minutes, or until tender.

Serve the fish piping hot, in their loosely opened packets.

stir-fried beef & snow peas

very easy   serves 4

10 minutes   10 minutes

ingredients

1 lb/450 g round or sirloin steak,
  sliced thinly
2 tbsp soy sauce
5 tbsp hoisin sauce
2 tbsp dry sherry
vegetable oil spray
1 onion, sliced thinly
1 tsp chopped fresh garlic
1 tsp chopped fresh ginger

1 carrot, sliced thinly
1 lb/450 g snow peas
8 oz/225 g canned sliced bamboo shoots,
  drained

cooked rice or noodles, to serve

NUTRITIONAL INFORMATION	
calories	249
protein	33 g
carbohydrate	15 g
sugars	12 g
fat	6 g
saturates	2 g

Put the strips of beef in a bowl, add the soy sauce, hoisin sauce, and sherry and stir together. Let marinate while you are cooking the vegetables.

Spray a large nonstick wok with oil. Add the onion, garlic, ginger, carrot, and snow peas and stir-fry for 5 minutes, or until softened.

Add the beef and marinade to the wok and stir-fry for 2–3 minutes, or until tender. Add the bamboo shoots and stir-fry for a further minute, until hot.

Transfer to a warm serving dish, and serve with cooked rice or noodles, if you like.

bœuf stroganoff

very easy   serves 4

5 minutes   15 minutes

vegetable oil spray
1 onion, sliced coarsely
3¼ cups thinly sliced white mushrooms
1 tsp French mustard
1 lb/450 g round or sirloin steak,
  sliced thinly

1¼ cups reduced-fat crème fraîche
salt and pepper

chopped fresh parsley, to garnish

NUTRITIONAL INFORMATION	
calories	302
protein	30 g
carbohydrate	7 g
sugars	5 g
fat	17 g
saturates	11 g

Spray a large, nonstick skillet with oil. Add the onion and cook, stirring, for 5 minutes, until softened and lightly colored.

Add the mushrooms and mustard to the skillet and cook, stirring occasionally, for a further 4–5 minutes, or until lightly colored.

Add the beef to the skillet and cook, stirring occasionally, for 5 minutes, or until tender. Add the crème fraîche and salt and pepper, then heat, stirring constantly, until hot.

Serve garnished with parsley.

linguine with shrimp

very easy serves 4

5 minutes 15 minutes

ingredients

12 oz/350 g linguine
salt and pepper
1 tbsp white wine vinegar
1 tbsp lemon juice
2 tbsp tomato paste
pinch of sugar
6 tbsp water

1 tsp chopped fresh garlic
1 tsp chopped fresh ginger
2 cups peeled cooked shrimp
4 scallions, sliced thinly

chopped fresh parsley, to garnish

NUTRITIONAL INFORMATION	
calories	359
protein	21 g
carbohydrate	68 g
sugars	5 g
fat	2 g
saturates	0 g

Cook the pasta in a large pan of boiling salted water for 10 minutes, or as directed on the package, until tender.

Meanwhile, put the vinegar, lemon juice, tomato paste, sugar, water, salt, and pepper in a bowl and mix together.

Put the garlic, ginger, shrimp, and scallions in a large, heavy nonstick skillet and heat gently for 1–2 minutes, stirring constantly, until hot.

Drain the cooked pasta and add to the skillet. Combine with the sauce mixture and heat, stirring, until the pasta is well coated and the sauce is heated through.

Serve garnished with parsley.

moussaka

easy serves 4

40 minutes 45 minutes

ingredients

2 eggplants, sliced thinly
1 lb/450 g lean ground beef
2 onions, sliced thinly
1 tsp finely chopped garlic
14 oz/400 g canned tomatoes

2 tbsp chopped fresh parsley
salt and pepper
2 eggs
1¼ cups lowfat plain yogurt
1 tbsp grated Parmesan cheese

NUTRITIONAL INFORMATION	
calories	357
protein	36 g
carbohydrate	17 g
sugars	15 g
fat	16 g
saturates	7 g

In a large nonstick skillet, dry-fry the eggplant slices, in batches, on both sides until brown. Remove from the skillet.

Add the beef to the pan and cook for 5 minutes, stirring, until browned. Stir in the onions and garlic and cook for 5 minutes, or until lightly browned. Add the tomatoes, parsley, salt, and pepper, then bring the mixture to a boil, and simmer for 20 minutes, or until the meat is tender.

Preheat the oven to 350°F/180°C. Arrange half the eggplant slices in a layer in an ovenproof dish. Add the meat mixture, then a final layer of the remaining eggplant slices.

In a bowl, beat the eggs, then beat in the yogurt, and add salt and pepper. Pour the mixture over the eggplants and sprinkle the grated cheese on top. Bake the moussaka in the oven for 45 minutes, or until golden brown. Serve straight from the dish.

marinated lamb kabobs

very easy   serves 4

10 minutes   15–20
+ 2–3 hours   minutes
to marinate

MARINADE
⅔ cup lowfat plain yogurt
4 tbsp chopped fresh cilantro
2 tsp chopped garlic
2 tsp chopped fresh ginger
1 tsp ground coriander
1 tsp ground cumin
salt and pepper

1 lb/450 g leg of lamb, cut into
    1-inch/2.5-cm cubes

chopped fresh parsley, to garnish

salad, to serve

NUTRITIONAL INFORMATION	
calories	200
protein	25 g
carbohydrate	3 g
sugars	3 g
fat	10 g
saturates	4 g

Put all the marinade ingredients into a large bowl and mix together. Stir in the lamb until coated in the marinade, then marinate in the refrigerator for 2–3 hours.

Thread the lamb cubes onto metal or bamboo skewers. Cook under a preheated broiler for 15–20 minutes, turning frequently and basting with the marinade, until tender.

Garnish with parsley and serve with salad.

quick-fried pork & pears

very easy   serves 4

15 minutes   5–7 minutes

i n g r e d i e n t s

1 tbsp soy sauce

1 tsp white wine vinegar

2 tbsp dry sherry

1 lb/450 g pork tenderloin,
  sliced very thinly

2 large pears

4 scallions, sliced thinly

1 tsp chopped garlic

1 tbsp chopped fresh ginger

NUTRITIONAL INFORMATION	
calories	210
protein	25 g
carbohydrate	9 g
sugars	8 g
fat	7 g
saturates	2 g

Put the soy sauce, vinegar, and sherry in a large bowl. Add the pork and mix together. Cut the pears into ¼-inch/5-mm slices, discarding the cores.

Reserve the green part of the scallions to use as garnish. Put the garlic, ginger, and scallions in a large nonstick wok and heat for 1–2 minutes, stirring constantly, until hot.

Add the pork mixture to the wok and stir-fry for 3–4 minutes, or until tender and beginning to brown. Add the pears and stir-fry for a further minute, or until hot.

Serve the stir-fry immediately, sprinkled with the sliced green scallion stems.

Vegetables are the perfect healthy food and in this section is a collection of recipes using just vegetables as a main course. They illustrate how interesting and varied vegetables can be, but fortunately you don't have to be a vegetarian to enjoy them! You will find healthy recipes for Cheese & Spinach Lasagna, Vegetable Biryani, Glazed Vegetable Kabobs, and Stuffed Eggplants, among other delicious dishes. Their flavor and freshness have been brought out to the full to provide nutritious and satisfying meals.

vegetarian
dishes

spring vegetable risotto

easy   serves 4

15 minutes   30–35
             minutes

ingredients

3¾ cups vegetable bouillon
2 tsp olive oil
1 small leek, sliced thinly
1 tsp chopped garlic
1 carrot, sliced thinly
2 zucchini, sliced thinly
¾ cup snow peas

¾ cup whole green beans,
   cut into 1-inch/2.5-cm pieces
3 cups risotto rice
⅔ cup dry white wine
½ cup frozen baby
   peas, thawed
salt and pepper

NUTRITIONAL INFORMATION	
calories	429
protein	10 g
carbohydrate	36 g
sugars	14 g
fat	16 g
saturates	9 g

Pour the bouillon into a pan, bring to a boil, then keep at barely simmering point.

Meanwhile, heat the oil in a large nonstick pan, add the leek, garlic, carrot, zucchini, snow peas, and beans and cook, stirring frequently, for 5 minutes, or until beginning to soften but not brown.

Add the rice and stir well for 2–3 minutes, or until coated in the oil. Add the wine and cook, stirring, until almost evaporated.

Add about ⅔ cup of the bouillon and cook gently, stirring occasionally, until absorbed. Add more bouillon, in ⅔ cup measures, as soon as each measure has been absorbed, stirring frequently. Continue until the rice is thick, creamy, and tender. This will take 20–25 minutes. Stir in the peas, season with salt and pepper, and serve.

cheese & spinach lasagna

very easy   serves 4

15 minutes   45–50
             minutes

1 lb/450 g frozen spinach, thawed
salt and pepper
2 cups lowfat ricotta cheese
8 sheets no-precook lasagne
2¼ cups strained bottled tomatoes

8 oz/225 g reduced fat mozzarella cheese,
 sliced thinly
1 tbsp freshly grated Parmesan cheese

salad (optional), to serve

NUTRITIONAL INFORMATION	
calories	369
protein	23 g
carbohydrate	36 g
sugars	14 g
fat	16 g
saturates	9 g

Preheat the oven to 350°F/180°C.

Put the spinach in a strainer and squeeze out as much excess liquid as possible.
Put half in the bottom of an ovenproof dish and add salt and pepper.

Spread half the ricotta over the spinach, cover with half the lasagna sheets, then
spoon over half the strained bottled tomatoes. Arrange half the mozzarella slices
on top. Repeat the layers and finally sprinkle over the Parmesan cheese.

Bake in the oven for 45–50 minutes, by which time the top should be brown
and bubbling.

Serve with salad, if you like.

pasta with ricotta & sun-dried tomatoes

very easy   serves 4

10 minutes   10 minutes

12 oz/350 g dried tagliatelle
salt and pepper
2 cups sun-dried tomatoes
 in oil, drained
1¾ cups lowfat ricotta cheese
1 garlic clove, crushed

TO GARNISH
freshly grated Parmesan cheese
fresh basil leaves

NUTRITIONAL INFORMATION	
calories	542
protein	18 g
carbohydrate	74 g
sugars	8 g
fat	22 g
saturates	6 g

Cook the pasta in a large pan of boiling salted water for 10 minutes or as directed on the package, until tender.

Meanwhile, using scissors, cut the tomatoes into small pieces into a pan. Add the ricotta, garlic, salt, and pepper and heat very gently, without boiling.

Drain the pasta, add to the tomato mixture, and toss together.

Serve garnished with basil leaves and generously sprinkled with freshly grated Parmesan.

penne primavera

very easy   serves 4

10 minutes 20 minutes

ingredients

1 cup baby corn
½ cup whole baby carrots
salt and pepper
1¼ cups shelled fava beans
generous 1 cup whole green beans,
   cut into 1-inch/2.5-cm pieces

3 cups dried penne
1¼ cups lowfat plain yogurt
1 tbsp chopped fresh parsley
1 tbsp chopped fresh chives

a few fresh chives, to garnish

NUTRITIONAL INFORMATION	
calories	398
protein	19 g
carbohydrate	79 g
sugars	11 g
fat	3 g
saturates	1 g

Cook the corn and carrots in boiling salted water for 5 minutes, or until tender, then drain, and rinse under cold running water. Cook the fava beans and green beans in boiling salted water for 3–4 minutes, or until tender, then drain, and rinse under cold running water. If you like, slip the skins off the fava beans.

Cook the pasta in a large pan of boiling salted water for 10 minutes, or as directed on the package, until tender.

Meanwhile, put the yogurt, parsley, chopped chives, salt, and pepper in a bowl and mix together.

Drain the cooked pasta and return to the pan. Add the vegetables and yogurt sauce, heat gently, and toss together, until hot.

Serve garnished with a few lengths of chives.

vegetable biryani

very easy

serves 4

10 minutes

30 minutes

1 onion, cut into fourths
2 garlic cloves
1 tsp chopped fresh gingerroot
1 tsp ground coriander
1 tsp ground cumin
1 tsp ground turmeric
½ tsp chili powder
salt and pepper
6¼ cups water
2 carrots, sliced thickly

1½ cups whole green beans,
   cut into 1-inch/2.5-cm lengths
½ cauliflower head, cut into florets
1¾ cups basmati rice
2 whole cloves
¼ tsp cardamom seeds
2 tbsp lime juice

chopped fresh cilantro, to garnish

NUTRITIONAL INFORMATION	
calories	378
protein	11 g
carbohydrate	80 g
sugars	8 g
fat	2 g
saturates	0 g

Put the onion, garlic, ginger, coriander, cumin, turmeric, chili, salt, and pepper in a food processor and process until smooth.

Spoon the spice mixture into a large nonstick pan and cook, stirring, for 2 minutes. Stir in 3¾ cups of the water and bring to a boil. Add the carrots, beans, and cauliflower and simmer for 15 minutes, or until tender.

Meanwhile, put the rice in a strainer and rinse under cold running water. Put in a pan with the remaining 2½ cups of water, the cloves, cardamom seeds, and salt. Bring to a boil, then simmer for 10 minutes, or until just tender.

Drain the rice and stir into the vegetables with the lime juice. Simmer gently until the rice is tender and the liquid has been absorbed. Serve garnished with cilantro.

bean & vegetable chili

very easy   serves 4

10 minutes   20 minutes

ingredients

4 tbsp vegetable bouillon
1 onion, chopped coarsely
1 green bell pepper, seeded
  and chopped finely
1 red bell pepper, seeded
  and chopped finely
1 tsp finely chopped garlic
1 tsp finely chopped fresh ginger
2 tsp ground cumin
½ tsp chili powder

2 tbsp tomato paste
14 oz/400 g canned chopped tomatoes
salt and pepper
14 oz/400 g canned kidney beans, drained
14 oz/400 g canned black-eye
  peas, drained

chopped fresh cilantro, to garnish

fresh crusty bread, to serve

NUTRITIONAL INFORMATION	
calories	246
protein	17 g
carbohydrate	44 g
sugars	14 g
fat	2 g
saturates	0 g

Heat the bouillon in a large pan, add the onion and bell peppers and simmer for 5 minutes, or until softened.

Stir in the garlic, ginger, cumin, chili powder, tomato paste, tomatoes (together with their juice), salt, and pepper and simmer for 10 minutes. Stir in the kidney beans and black-eye peas and simmer for a further 5 minutes, or until hot. Remove the pan from the heat and transfer the chili to a warm serving dish.

Garnish with chopped cilantro and serve with fresh crusty bread.

glazed vegetable kabobs

very easy   serves 4

15 minutes   10 minutes

ingredients

⅔ cup lowfat plain yogurt
4 tbsp mango chutney
1 tsp chopped garlic
1 tbsp lemon juice
salt and pepper
8 baby onions, peeled

16 baby corn, halved
2 zucchini, cut into
   1-inch/2.5-cm pieces
16 white mushrooms
16 cherry tomatoes

salad greens, to garnish

NUTRITIONAL INFORMATION	
calories	144
protein	8 g
carbohydrate	26 g
sugars	24 g
fat	1 g
saturates	0 g

Put the yogurt, chutney, garlic, lemon juice, salt, and pepper in a bowl and stir together.

Put the onions in a pan of boiling water. Return to a boil, then drain well.

Thread the onions, corn, zucchini, mushrooms, and tomatoes alternately onto 8 metal or bamboo skewers.

Arrange the kabobs on a broiler pan and brush with the yogurt glaze. Cook under a preheated broiler for 10 minutes, turning and brushing frequently, until golden and tender.

Serve with a garnish of mixed salad greens.

stuffed eggplants

easy   serves 4

15 minutes   45 minutes

ingredients

2 eggplants
1 onion, chopped finely
1 tsp chopped garlic
1½ cups coarsely chopped
 white mushrooms

2 tsp chopped fresh cilantro
1 cup fresh bread crumbs
salt and pepper
2 oz/55 g feta cheese (drained weight),
 crumbled finely

NUTRITIONAL INFORMATION	
calories	104
protein	5 g
carbohydrate	13 g
sugars	5 g
fat	4 g
saturates	2 g

Put the eggplants in a large pan of boiling water and cook for 20 minutes, or until tender. Drain well.

Cut the eggplants in half lengthwise, scoop out the flesh, and chop finely. Reserve the eggplant shells.

Preheat the oven to 350°F/180°C.

Put the eggplant flesh, onion, garlic, mushrooms, and cilantro in a nonstick skillet and cook for 5 minutes. Stir in the bread crumbs, salt, and pepper.

Stuff the eggplant shells with the mixture and sprinkle with the feta cheese.

Place on a cookie sheet and bake in the oven for 20 minutes. Transfer to warm serving plates and serve immediately.

The healthy pudding and dessert recipes in this chapter use fresh or dried fruits and are bursting with tempting flavors. There is a selection of both hot puddings and cold desserts, such as Apple Strudel with Warm Cider Sauce, Apricot & Orange Fool, and Raspberry Creams. Tropical Fruit Salad is a simple and refreshing dessert dressed with your choice of fresh fruit juice. You will find that all these recipes will bring an enjoyable finale to any meal.

puddings
& desserts

golden baked apple pudding

very easy   serves 4

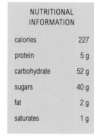

15 minutes   30–35
minutes

ingredients

1 lb/450 g cooking apples
1 tsp ground cinnamon
2 tbsp golden raisins
4 oz/115 g whole-wheat bread

generous ½ cup lowfat
  cottage cheese
4 tbsp light brown sugar
generous 1 cup lowfat milk

NUTRITIONAL INFORMATION	
calories	227
protein	5 g
carbohydrate	52 g
sugars	40 g
fat	2 g
saturates	1 g

Preheat the oven to 425°F/220°C.

Peel and core the apples and chop the flesh into ½-inch/1-cm pieces. Put the apple pieces in a bowl and toss with the cinnamon and golden raisins.

Remove the crusts and cut the bread into ½-inch/1-cm cubes. Add to the apples with the cottage cheese and 3 tablespoons of the brown sugar, and mix together. Stir in the milk.

Turn the mixture into an ovenproof dish and sprinkle with the remaining sugar. Bake in the oven for 30–35 minutes, or until golden brown. Serve hot.

apricot & orange fool

extremely easy

serves 4

5 minutes

ingredients

generous 1 cup ready-to-eat
  dried apricots
1 tbsp honey
generous 1 cup fresh orange juice
generous 1 cup lowfat
  plain yogurt

2 tsp flaked almonds (toasted),
  to decorate

NUTRITIONAL INFORMATION	
calories	171
protein	6 g
carbohydrate	37 g
sugars	37 g
fat	1 g
saturates	0 g

Put all the ingredients, except the almonds, in a food processor and process until smooth.

Serve in individual glass dishes, decorated with toasted almonds.

spiced baked pears

extremely
easy

serves 4

5 minutes   30 minutes

ingredients

4 large, firm eating pears
⅔ cup apple juice
1 cinnamon stick

4 whole cloves
1 bay leaf

NUTRITIONAL INFORMATION	
calories	114
protein	1 g
carbohydrate	29 g
sugars	29 g
fat	0 g
saturates	0 g

Preheat the oven to 350°F/180°C.

Peel and core the pears and cut them into quarters. Place in an ovenproof dish and add the remaining ingredients.

Cover the dish and bake in the oven for 30 minutes.

Serve the pears hot or cold.

apple strudel with warm cider sauce

easy   serves 2–4

25 minutes   15–20 minutes

8 crisp eating apples
1 tbsp lemon juice
⅔ cup golden raisins
1 tsp ground cinnamon
½ tsp grated nutmeg
1 tbsp light brown sugar
6 sheets phyllo pastry
vegetable oil spray

SAUCE
1 tbsp cornstarch
2 cups hard cider

confectioners' sugar, to serve

NUTRITIONAL INFORMATION	
calories	283
protein	3 g
carbohydrate	61 g
sugars	47 g
fat	1 g
saturates	0 g

Preheat the oven to 375°F/190°C. Line a cookie sheet with nonstick liner.

Peel and core the apples and chop them into ½-inch/1-cm dice. Toss the pieces in a bowl with the lemon juice, golden raisins, cinnamon, nutmeg, and sugar.

Lay out a sheet of phyllo, spray with vegetable oil, and lay a second sheet on top. Repeat with a third sheet. Spread over half the apple mixture and roll up lengthwise, tucking in the ends to enclose the filling. Repeat to make a second strudel. Slide onto the cookie sheet, spray with oil, and bake for 15–20 minutes.

Blend the cornstarch in a pan with a little hard cider until smooth. Add the remaining cider and heat gently, stirring, until the mixture boils and thickens. Serve the strudel warm or cold, dredged with confectioners' sugar and accompanied by the cider sauce.

tropical fruit salad

very easy   serves 4

20 minutes   none
+ 1 hour to
chill

ingredients

1 ripe mango
1 papaya
1 small pineapple

1¼ cups pineapple
   or orange juice
2 small bananas

NUTRITIONAL INFORMATION	
calories	154
protein	2 g
carbohydrate	38 g
sugars	37 g
fat	1 g
saturates	0 g

Cutting close to the pit, cut a large slice from one side of the mango, then cut another slice from the opposite side. Without breaking the skin, cut the flesh in the segments into squares, then push the skin inside out to expose the cubes, and cut away from the skin. Use a sharp knife to peel the remaining center section and cut the flesh away from the pit into cubes. Reserve any juice and put in a serving bowl with the mango flesh.

Cut the papaya in half and discard the seeds. Remove the skin and cut the flesh into cubes. Peel the pineapple, remove the center core and as many "eyes" as possible, and cut the flesh into chunks. Add both fruits to the mango.

Pour in the fruit juice and chill the mixture in the refrigerator for about 1 hour. Just before serving, slice the bananas and add the slices to the fruit salad.

apple & honey water ice

very easy   serves 4

10 minutes   20 minutes
+ 5–6 hours
to freeze

ingredients

4 crisp eating apples
2 tbsp lemon juice
scant 1 cup water

5 tbsp sugar
2 tbsp honey

apple slices, to decorate

NUTRITIONAL INFORMATION	
calories	175
protein	0 g
carbohydrate	46 g
sugars	46 g
fat	0 g
saturates	0 g

Peel and core the apples and cut them into chunks. Put in a pan with the lemon juice and 1 tablespoon of water and heat gently for about 20 minutes, stirring frequently, until soft.

Meanwhile, put the sugar and the remaining water in a pan and heat gently, stirring, until dissolved. Bring to a boil, then boil for 2 minutes. Remove from the heat.

Push the apple through a strainer into a bowl. Stir in the sugar syrup and honey. Let stand until cold.

When cold, pour the mixture into a freezer container. Freeze, uncovered, for 2 hours, until the water ice mixture begins to set. Turn the mixture into a bowl and whisk until smooth. Return to the container and freeze for a further 3–4 hours until firm.

Serve decorated with apple slices.

raspberry creams

very easy   serves 4

10 minutes   none
+ 1 hour
to chill

2⅔ cups raspberries
¾ cup lowfat cottage cheese
3 tbsp sugar
⅔ cup lowfat plain yogurt

confectioners' sugar, to decorate

NUTRITIONAL INFORMATION	
calories	142
protein	9 g
carbohydrate	25 g
sugars	25 g
fat	1 g
saturates	1 g

Reserving a few whole raspberries to decorate, use the back of a spoon to push the raspberries and cottage cheese through a strainer into a bowl.

Stir the sugar and yogurt into the raspberry mixture and stir to blend, then spoon into individual serving dishes. Chill in the refrigerator for about 1 hour.

Serve chilled, decorated with the reserved raspberries and dusted with sifted confectioners' sugar.

compote of dried fruit

extremely easy   serves 4

25 minutes
+ 24 hours
to marinate   none

ingredients

1 tbsp jasmine tea
1¼ cups boiling water
¼ cup dried apricots

¼ cup dried apple rings
¼ cup prunes
1¼ cups fresh orange juice

NUTRITIONAL INFORMATION	
calories	103
protein	2 g
carbohydrate	25 g
sugars	25 g
fat	0 g
saturates	0 g

Put the tea in a pitcher and pour in the boiling water. Let steep for 20 minutes, then strain.

Put the dried fruits in a serving bowl and pour the jasmine tea and orange juice over them. Cover and marinate in the refrigerator for 24 hours.

Serve the compote well chilled.

compote of dried fruit

extremely
easy

serves 4

25 minutes
+ 24 hours
to marinate

ingredients

1 tbsp jasmine tea

1¼ cups boiling water

¼ cup dried apricots

¼ cup dried apple rings

¼ cup prunes

1¼ cups fresh orange juice

NUTRITIONAL INFORMATION	
calories	103
protein	2 g
carbohydrate	25 g
sugars	25 g
fat	0 g
saturates	0 g

Put the tea in a pitcher and pour in the boiling water. Let steep for 20 minutes, then strain.

Put the dried fruits in a serving bowl and pour the jasmine tea and orange juice over them. Cover and marinate in the refrigerator for 24 hours.

Serve the compote well chilled.

index